I0139217

echoes from hell

Scott Shaw

Buddha Rose Publications

echoes from hell
Copyright © 1988 by Scott Shaw
www.scottshaw.com
ALL RIGHTS RESERVED

First Edition 1988
Second Edition 2013

No part of this book may be reproduced in any manner without the expressed written permission of the author or the publishing company.

Library of Congress Catalog Card Number: 2013950393

ISBN: 1-877792-71-3
ISBN-13: 978-1-877792-71-7

10 9 8 7 6 5 4 3 2 1

Printed in the United States of America

echoes from hell

contents

introduction

Most people are sucked in-to the reality of maintaining a day-to-day existence. When they are young they must go to school so that they can someday find a, *"Good Job."* Once they are of employable age their entire life-focus shift(s) to their job – all of their thoughts, hopes dreams, ambitions are focused upon that source of income. They must work hard to pay for where they live/how they live. They must maintain employment so that they can lure the appropriate mate into their life and live in the Happily-Every-After world of illusion.

By the way, Where is that place?

In any case, once they have met that perfect mate, they must then have kid(s) so that they can live out all of their unfulfilled dreams/fantasies through those children. *"I want little Sally or little Jimmy's life to be better than mine…"* But, all that happens is that their children go to school in order to get a good job, so that the whole process of expressing another meaning(less) life can be actualized in its entirely unfulfilling-ness *over and over and over* again. Many would say, *"This is just the way it is…"* I don't believe that.

Let's take a moment and look at you. Who did you want to become? Did following the path that was laid out before you equal that dream? If it did, then *all is well with the world.* If it did not, there is a problem.

Some feel… Probably the type of person who would read a book of verse like this believe(s) that, *"Art,"* was/is their calling. And, *"The World,"* and the way it is structured, (in many cases), keeps them from living their life to the full abstraction of that art. Maybe/Probably…

But, let's face facts. *Artists,* (of what-ever kind), have fought against society to find their niche since the dawning of the age of enlightenment. Some, (a very few), have, in fact, found their way to financial and critical success from their desired *Art-Form.* Most have not, however. But, at the heart of what an artist chooses to do, is THEIR-ART. Whether they become: *"Renown," "Successful," "Financial Solvent,"* from their *Art-Form* or not, is not the issue. <u>Art is the issue.</u>

What artists have done, from the beginning of time forward, is to lay a foundation for what is not currently accepted but what could/should/may-be accepted. What an artist does is to illustrate a new/different reality that can/may be experienced only by a select few. In doing so, they set about on detailing a new understanding of *LIFE* and of *REALITY.*

Whether loved or hated, embraced, understood, (or not), this has never been the issue. What the artist does is LIVE. By living and creating in an abstract reality, (that is not commonly embraced or rarely even understood by the masses), they continue/they aid in the evolution of human consciousness and the explanation(s) thereof.

Goddamn, this sounds like philosophy! It is not! It is simply an explanation of *Life* and of *Life-Reality*. A reality lived by me and by other artists. Those of us who exist out here in the *Out-Back;* out here on the *Out-Skirts.*

What must be understood/comprehended is that this, *"Outer Realm,"* is where ART, (for lack of any better term), is known/is embraced/is created.

In the words that follow this meaningless little introductory discourse, allow me to dance your minds into the realms of, *The Art of Blatant Reality* – at least as I have lived it/experienced it. Allow me to transcribe a few words I wrote about a few situation(s) that artfully entered my life out there/here on the outskirts of reality – the abstract reality not known or accepted by the masses.

Maybe that's it! Maybe that's the definition! The definition of, *"Art,"* that is… It is, *"The not accepted…"* At least the not accepted/understood yet – right now. We can all hope, maybe someday it will be…

I mean, let's face facts: church, state, schools, gurus, priests, and professors, they all tell you how you are suppose to feel – what you are suppose to do. They tell you what is RIGHT with them and WRONG with you. They detail what is,

"The Way," explained by whom-ever wrote what-ever book they claim to be holy. Fuck that!

Art is not holy. Not by their standard(s) anyway… Art is only known by the few who have/who do LIVE IT. Not by those who claim to know something that they do not and then attempt to teach what they have not experienced.

So, as I always exclaim, *"Live the art!"*

Art is living.

Here are a few words about that living and the price you pay to do/experience the said.

Scott Shaw
December 1988
Redondo Beach, California

verse

I have a watch
    rolex
    it says upon its dial
and
if you pull
the time set knob out
    out
    all the way
then its ticking stops
    time stops
I sit in a restaurant
a restaurant of choice
    a dream in the making
    a place to create
my mind works
my body eats
I have come here
for several years now
    it was a day
    like today
    a day, I think
    two weeks ago
    I sat in the dream
    I sat awaiting a dream
    I pull my watch's time set knob out
    and for a second or two
    time stopped

it is sad
how much it doesn't matter anymore
        dug in too deep
        lies, there have been a lot told
        love, it hurts
        and there never seems to be a way out

so I sit here
basking in all this artistic freedom
lavishing in all this artistic pain
and it doesn't mean a god damned thing
it doesn't breed a thing
        only the more of the nothing
        only the zero
        and all that is done
                is none

        it would all be too much untruth
        if I said
        I wished it wasn't different
                a dream fulfilled
                a goal gained
                a memory shared
                something/anything
                one more time

but the words go on and on
time ticks on and on

and every dream
well, it fades to every lie
and every reason
well, it just doesn't seem to matter anymore
    the dollars I spend
    the letters I send
    the life I pretend
    nothing, nothing, nothing

in the ghettos
in the slums
the mind plays tricks on the eyes

in the streets
life is hard
life is short
it never lasts too long

light(s) reflection
light(s) her eyes
light(s) call out
into the night

I know them well
too well
      the light
      the night
      her nighttime eyes

too well
      they make me run away

the feeling(s)
it/they are all the same

now I am gone
now I am older

older than I was
yesterday

nowhere to run
no more tears to cry
fire into fire
the light call me out into the night

nowhere left to run
yet still, I run away
        into the slow
        into the ghetto
        into the streets

it's called religion
and it changes everything in sight
the name is called religion
and it changes everything in the night

reality
I have heard people
speak about it
but personality
I have never met it

six

I remember
how the night cried
while searching for a dream worth living

I remember
the night(s)
spent dreaming
while living the lie

I remember
the drunken nights of bliss
holding each other
        all night long

and I remember
the nights
spend all alone

mostly, I remember the desire
        desire
        that the dream(s)
        would all be something more
        that life would mean something
        but it/they do not

        yes, I remember

listen
as the kiss
become midnight

listen
as the dream
of love dies

listen
to all the memories

listen
to all the fantasies

listen as tomorrow's dream
speaks

I cried
oh yes
I have cried

listen
to the love
that could be
that has not been

but maybe tomorrow...
      oh yes
      there is always tomorrow

listen
as all the drunken poets speak
      talking all of their lies

      listen to the fantasy
      listen to the dream
      listen to the perfection
      listen
      yes, listen

distant glance
in the mirror

distance
glances
in its own way

and all that is
is that this has become
and tonight
well, it promises everything

nine

To Scott —

I promise to never fool around
and to be together forever and ever.

Beverly

2-18-88

to all the women
who draw in my notebook(s)
and make promise they can't keep
promises I don't want them to make…

it was all so long ago
    it seems
    too long ago
    to even matter anymore

        back then
        back
        when the dreams were clear

do you still have them?
the dream that were way back when?

it all seemed so haveable
an answer
    to it all
it all seemed
    like it would come
where did it go?

        faded into night's alone
        nights
        when
        life
        just hurts too much
            just hurts too much to dream

faded into the running away
      running away
      from the pain
somewhere/anywhere
      where it just
      wouldn't hurt anymore

now, they say
a coward cries a coward's tears
and a liar is destine to lie
but when the wave of suchness
smashes you in the face
when the splash of insecurity
hits too hard
      too many times
then anyone
would run and hide

so where are they now
where are the dreams
that were promised
      the dreams
      that were dreamt

faded into this night
I guess…
      faded
      as this night fades on

eleven

why do you never help
to solve the problems
why do you only aid
in the creation of them?
      questions asked of me

lost
the moments spin
into the severed wind
that blows
through this night's sky

reminiscences
of days gone past
years gone by
      past
      just the same…

      lost
      am I never to be
      who I once was
      or is it simply
      that I have changed
         and all that
         all of who I used to be
         just doesn't matter anymore

lost
in the world
a world of a woman
a woman
I love
a woman
the kind
that I could never love

but she pulls me back in
show me where I once was
makes me feel vacant
for not remaining there

all the same
that time is gone
who I was is gone

so why do you continue
to create the problem(s)
why do you never give the answer
to them being solved
and the weight
becomes heavier
on my shoulders
the weight
becomes heavier
on my mind

twelve

I was there
when she cried
woven
her tears of pain
tears of confidence
tears of love

I was there
when she cried
cried her tears of lies

I was there
I believed them
    like the fool I am

      how could the tears
      fall so freely
      run down her cheeks
      so believably
      yet so full of lies

I was there
when she cried
woven
full of lies
as she cried
I believed them
I don't believe them now

there have been a lot of times
times like these
when I stare deep
inside the walls
which surround me

     surround me
     enclose me
     trap me

but I have no way out
     no place
     left to run

I had a girl
a recent love
     love
     recently
but it/she held me
it/she bound me
it/she forced me to believe
forced me to lie
forced me to pretend
that I could forgive and forget
a destructive past
that I had nothing to do in creating

the walls
I saw them develop
I saw them
as I stared deeply into them
I thought for a moment
that she
may have been my way out
but she was only
a deeper way in
      deeper
      way in
      inside the walls

but me
it is I
I, who still pays the bills
of love
      for her
      and before her

the gifts I purchased
the lies I told
the dreams I laid
that broke
into a million pieces

the walls
they surround me

I've got nowhere left to run
      no money
      no time
      simply strained eyes
      that have gazed
      too long
      too deeply
      into the walls
      the walls that close in on me

           walls of no purity
           walls of no destiny
           walls laid by the hands
           of someone else
           but walls that sucked me in
               and trapped me
               just the same

fourteen

I spend a good part of my life
    doing what
    I don't want to do
    being what
    I don't want to be
    seeing what
    I don't want to see

life and time
and no direction
the world
that keeps pulling me down
    around and around
    into no connection
    living past
    the danger zone
but when there is no one to be
nothing left to see
and all the loves
have gone bad
    when there's no games to play
    no dreams to live
    and all the wasted time
    equals nothing at all
    then faith turns to truth
    truth turns to the knowledge
    that nothing means nothing
    then zen is ultimately understood

ten cents
for the innocents
it all adds up
to nothing at all

yes
ten cents
for the innocent
nothing means
nothing at all

      three months
      in place and time
      I gave them to you
      would you give them to me
         all seemed fine
         'till it added up to nothing
            and nothing
            means nothing at all

when the illusion lies
and the dream(s) rein supreme

where the dreamer dies
and the lovers cry
      the tears are shed
      for nothing
      no not anything at all

when the morning sun is broken
a million pieces of it
go flying by

when the morning sun is gone
you know
that life
it doesn't mean anything
no not anything at all

illusive
illusion
poetry
she sings to me
>yeah, she give me love
>she gives me a reason
>she gives me the few things
>that she has left to give

>I'll take it
>I'll take anything
>anything that keeps me going
>through the night

distant lady
san francisco
she sings to me
>flirtation
>beams from her eyes

the night is young
everywhere to go
everything is new
to be seen
>yes
>she give me momentary love
>a momentary dream
>and that is all I ask for

there's this place I go to
in san francisco
it's a little Italian joint
off of poke street

yeah, I know
that street is where faggots
sell their booties
like santa monica B.L.V.D.
        here in L.A.

but the restaurant has this nice little
outdoor patio
facing the streets
and you get some great
traditional
italian food
and some more than fine
italian red wine

when I make my
couple times a month
journey up that direction
it is my first source
of substance

they love me there
me, the guy who kills a bottle of the grape
        solo
eats some food
throws down a big tip
then heads out to the night

        you see
        this is the essence of life
        a place that gives you what you need

        in an atmosphere
        that stirs your artistic soul

                I have written many a verse there

then/there
the night is forever
so much to be had
once the intoxication is in place
once the surrounding
have promised the passion
of new vision
        a female form

and a city like
san francisco

where everything/anything
is possible

I live for place(s)
where anything/everything
is possible

she died her hair
dark blonde
it glistened in the night

asian eyes
I drunkenly
staggered up to her
    but me
    I'm cool
    I hold my alcohol well
    few ever know/realize
    how fucked up I actually/really am

the chick
she had style
       red
       she wore red
       not my favorite color
       but then I don't hate it either

my long blonde hair
it was pulled back tight
    tight
    yes
    tight

    she looked at me
    smiled

she ran her hand over my head
grabbed a hold of my pony tail
and pulled it just a little bit
         our fate was sealed

it was an art gallery
around us were people
         artist(s)
         or say they claim

         people selling the art that hung on the walls
         or, at least, so they tired

         waitresses cruising the floor
         glasses of champaign on their trays
                  thanks
                  I'll have one of those

we spoke a little bit
         the girl
         her and I
         but eventually
         I became too drunk to care
         what she had to say

let's go
we left
and the rest is history
      history that has been lived/told before

and yes
all the poetry
it comes from here/from her
created
by all the dreamers
who are willing to take a chance
in the night

all the drunkenly scribbled lines
that can/will never be read
      the all
      and the all

      of no-where
      of no-time
      of no-life
      of the nothing-left-to-lose

just a dream
that goes
to where no one else can see
      a touch
      it is worth everything

her touch
it cast an etching upon my soul

she
that girl
from the art gallery
in a san francisco night
yeah
she was the everything
I wish I remembered her name

in the distance
all that distance
all the places to be

and I have seen the tears
that you have had to cry
I too have cried a few

as the ringing of the nighttime
stretches into the distance
she gave anything
that I would take

would you like to be in love ?
no thanks
oh well…

she questioned
I answered
the conversation was over

and when you are in this space
the space
within time/without time
when you are anywhere
where the rules just do not matter
that's the place for the free to dance

yeah, and…
she gives me her days off
days off
from her time
spent in the real world

I like blondes
she said
I laughed…

so anything is anything
when nothing
isn't anything at all

when every/any kiss
doesn't need to equal
anything
just a moment spent
in this moment
            yes, thank you
            I will take it

            life and love
            in your spare time
                    distance
                    cast to the distance

love and lust
shoot to kill
give it to me on a platter
and fire at will

who me?
I am nothing
      just a dreamer
      who still dreams
      about wishes
      he wishes to come true

and all that is dreamed
is all that is felt
and all that could be
is all that is created
      created in a mind

      creation
      the ultimate illusion
      as every lie
      is blended with every truth

so I listen to her
as she sing to me her sorrows
      every lie
      she tells me
      I try to believe that it is true
            but I know
            that it is not

so this is for you
for all the mystic dreamers

who dream of something else
that they are something else
      for all those dreams
      I have dreamed them too
      and all the lies
      I have hoped for them to be true
          yeah, the lies
          I know them all too well
          I have heard them/told them
          too many times

so sing to me
all you mystic dreamers
who have never succeeded
but try and try and try
      to make creation(s)
      a life
      your life
      an art

I listen to you
if no one else will
'cause I understand
a life lived
up against the wall

when you see the straight
see it as illusion
      the drunkard
      sees it as a dream

      the fool
      sees it as a meaning

      and the mystic
      finds it as a reason to scream

and when all the names
of form and finance
are lost
to the reason(s) of questioning why
and when nothing stands
      for anything
not anything at all
      than it is the truth
          the truth
          the truth that be known

and all that is seen
is all that is lost
for an existence
in never-never-land

and life
it doesn't mean anything at all

no, it will not free you
no, it will not save you
and no,
even living with everything
doesn't mean anything
no anything at all

just another one of those dreams
as I face the pacific ocean
drive to her
      down a hill

just another one of those dreams
paris
its been two years, maybe more
      I need to see her again

just one of those dreams
the kind that I want to live
      want to live
      can I live?
            money controls us all

so dream
mr. california
as you stand out on your balcony
atop the california sea

most would dream
to live as you do
      most dream
      to live as I do
      but my dreams
      they are all far-far away

just another one of those dreams
a month or so in paris
at that old hotel I love so much
        paint paintings
        paris on paper

        write words
        of dreams to live

        stare into the eyes
        of some unknown lover
                love
                yes, love

        but it is all
                just as it is
        a dream of the dreamer
        as he comes down
        that california hill

                the ocean it moves
                the sun it is setting
        and me
        I dream
        just another one of those dreams

if I only had the dollar(s)
the dollar(s) to pay for the dream(s)

if I only the dollar(s)
then I would not be lost
in this world of plastic passion
       that haunts
       the freedom
       of my days

& love it flows
& love it grows
       we held each other
       on the sand

& yes
it was magic
yes, it was the everything
       the everything
       that everybody dreams of
              yes
              it could be
              all that

but
like all life
like all love
it will escape us

& the tears they flow
as I look at her
     look deeply
         into her eyes

I see her dreams
I am her dreams
     dreams
         in all the lies

I see them
I have touched them
I have kissed them
I have fucked them
but they have been lies
just the same

no more lies
I say, no
no, I am not that/not your man

& now my lady
she sleeps
     sleeps
         in silence
     sleeps
         oblivious to the world

& she believes
that I am who I am
she believe that somehow/someway
she conjured me up
brought me to life
      summoned me out of her dreams

& it is all too much like the scene
a scene
so many years ago
      when a next-door neighbor girl
      cried for a gift
      the gift of me
         a gift
         she did not receive

         wanted to receive
           did not receive

& my thoughts drift to back then
to this still young man
      how she wanted me
      wanted it all
         wanted
         promises made forever
      wanted it now
      wanted it
      at any cost

well, the years
        they go by
on and on and on

me
functional
no

I'm a dreamer
but I have never beccme my dream

        want
        yes, I want

        which leads me to another story
        a story
        previously cast to the bastions of time...

I was twenty-five
she was seventeen
we sat in my porsche
waiting for our moment to begin

& in her innocence
innocence that faded all too fast
        faded years before
        she felt my my touch

in this moment of no moment
she spoke/she said,

you know, we don't have to do anything
we can do nothing
you don't have to entertain me
just being with you
is enough

why?
how could I ever be enough?

here/now
my lady/my love
she sleeps
     and she cries in her dreams
          tears roll down her face

          I see them
          I watch them
          as I write these words
          she cries in her sleep

for her
for them
for the love
I have tried to be
all that I am not

& truth and the lies
they confront me
dance with me
once again

      who I am
      what I am
         nothing
            no-thing
            again

so, quoting from my words written long ago
    any dream will do

      but, not I realize
      that's not true

love lost
& come again
it is like the slice of a razor
      a sharpened razor
      cutting me

      love
      causing
      only
      pain

so another night
        yes, it was love
        yes, it was magic

& me
I could/can never say, no

I get up
I walk over to the bed
I wipe her dreaming tears from her face
as she lays naked upon my sheets

        glad I'm your dream
        wish you could be mine

staring into the night
late night
mind warp
T.V.

     movies
     made a decade
     or two
     ago

     too much java
     can not sleep

     wasted love
     pulls my energy
     away from creativity

nothing worth watching
nothing better to do

     life and its paradox
     life and its time
     time, that ticks by

I look at myself
I wonder…
    where did I go wrong

    no…
    no regrets
    …nothing I would have done differently

    what then?

I guess the truth be known
I am just looking
    for something

        something
        that does not exist anymore

I take me
one last sip of the java
as the passion
fades to grey

       one more sip
       for one more night
       give me the juice
       artistic paradise

       where all the singers
       sing all the songs
       for all those
       whose life
       just went wrong

so sing it to me
one more time
       one more time
       as my life ticks on

sing it to me
for all the illusion
all the losing
all the not know knowing
       where to turn

all alone
and what do I do
when the near perfect
dream
dies

I've been drinking wine
for an hour or more
my brown rice
is almost done

two sides of a coin
two picture
different
       yet
       they turn out
       the same

first
and
last

present
and
past

where is there left to run

I purchased this wine
a year, two, maybe three ago

ten
fifteen year old
batch

      it is red
      for red
      improves with age

yes
it cost a dime or two

but that was then
         then
      when things were not so grim

      when I had
      a dime or two to spend

      when my plastic passions
      was not so deep

so I decide to pop its top

it is friday night
I drink

my phone rings
my machine answers it
>   my babe
>   my almost perfect dream
>   asian queen

almost should be CAPATILIZED

she says she is broken hearted/broken up
that she has not seen me

she asks
where am I
asia
san francisco
or just hiding out
and not answering my phone

yeah
I am hiding out
hiding out from her
hiding out from life
>   in these days
>   where I have no extra dimes to spend

hiding out
hiding out
and
waiting for the dream

     god, I need a dream
     god, I am tired of feeling this way

so drink on
drunken fool
cry your eyes out

watch T.V.
eat your brown rice
remember better days
when the dreams
were still haveable
and there was money
in your pocket

     remember:
     time to kill
     and money to spill

thirty

I need a shave
    in comparison
    with/to the way I feel

I need a shave
    in comparison
    with/to all that is around me

I need a shave
    in comparison

    but
    I shaved this morning

        my mind spins
        w/ the alcohol

        my apartment
        is a total mess

        my life
        it is in shambles
            nowhere to run
            no money to run with

I would cry
if I cried
but I don't

do you have
thirty seconds

    thirty seconds to live
        really live

so few
ever have the taste

    many may believe that they have
    many may claim that they have
        but they do not

play it cool
play it under the cuff
but play it
    as I play it still

    I drink
        still
    I live
        unstill
            even as age comes on

love
fame
lust
never-never-land

give it to me
because, yes
I have thirty seconds to live

failure
    I have decided
    that it is alright
    that I have failed

failure
    it is all around me
        lost dreams
        lost time
        lost to nothing
        but the passing illusion
        of life

failure
    yes
    my better days
    were so long ago

        so, now
        so, tonight
        I have decided
        to no longer
        tear myself up inside
        over what I have not accomplished
        over who I am not
            over and over
            the pain
            worse than failure

so I give up

      if I had a beer in the refrigerator
      I would drink it
      but I have finished
      all that were there

      so tomorrow
      I will run away
      go to san francisco
            go to s.f. from l.a.
      go
      and bask in my failure
      drink a good bottle of wine
      eat a good meal
            italian dinner
            on an outside patio
      and be glad
      that I lived long enough
      to fail

failure
      everyman's dream
      everyman's potential
            the source of all art

failure
      I have learned to love it

friday night
I sit back
to a glass of wine
a cup of coffee
T.V.

life, it has just gotten so boring

the glass of wine
goes down smooth
  fifteen years old
  and blood red

the java
to keep me awake
  a bit of a boost
  for a late night of writing

  the writing:
    look into the darkness
    the space in the time
    gone by
    a year here
    a moment there
    a song to remember
    and all the things
    that I wanted to be
    but did not become

it just seems
that there is not enough time

stay up all night
drink the wine
write the poetry
type the literature
coffee
it keeps me going

    now
    this is not to say
    that this is what
    I necessarily
    want to be doing
        nor is it to say
        that it is what I don't
        want to do

but the wine
gives freedom

the coffee
gives time

    the words
    speak to the ages

    and the literature
    is for the masses

so chastise me
if I am wrong
but I believe
that I have paid the price
       too long
       too much time
       too many dreams
       all equaling
       nothing

so
one more glass of wine
then back to the typing keys
one more cup of the java
to take the edge off
       keep the edge off

I do what I do
what else can I do?
but in truth
my dreams are elsewhere

thirty-five

I look at the shirt I wear
a shirt I took to tibet
    a shirt that I purchased
    in santa cruz

I give it a pull
and I say
in intoxicated silence to it

    we have to do
    something special again

it has now been
four, maybe five, almost six months
since I have been
out there on the hard road
    out of the country
too long
far too long
    between international dreams

    so give me a kiss for the silence
    give me a kiss for the lust
    give me a kiss for anything at all
    and I will travel to you
    yes, I will travel to you

so I'm going to kill
the one final
glass of wine
  glass of avoidance
  from the bottle

  a bottle of ten year old plus
  red/supreme

  yes, one more bottle down
  yes, one more time
  yes, lived in the alone
  of the dream/supreme

god, is that what I dreamed of
the life of a poet

it is hard to believe
how much I have lived it

  have I yet spent
  the required amount of time:
    of nights alone in misery
    of nights in question
    of nights in tears

alone/yes alone

and I wish I was in tokyo
and I wish I was bangkok
and I wish I was anywhere
but here in the no-where
　　　　　but no-where
　　　　　is all that I have

I laugh
I laugh to myself
　　　for all the I am not
　　　for all I can not be
　　　for all the hearts
　　　　　I have broken
　　　for all the life
　　　　　that has left me empty

　　　and lust
　　　I am so unfulfilled

　　　I laugh
　　　I laugh to myself
　　　in the all-alone

are my pains anymore
than the poets who have lived/walked before me

    the poets
    the artists
    the dreamers
    the messiahs
        I doubt it

pain
and poetry
they seem to go hand-in-hand

    and yes
    I say it
    once again
        I dream

    I dream of flying kites
    I dream of love
    I dream of asia
    I even dream of not being alone
           so alone

but that seems to be the price
the price that has to be paid

a price
so high
the price
for being the poet
the mystic

kiss me
kiss me goodnight
give me the kiss of fire
let me dream

thirty-eight

I have a chill
though the heater is on
     right in front of me

I have a chill
my bones vibrate

     the thought comes to my mind
        I may die

a chill in my bones
no way to get warm
     it scares me
     it scares me to death

now there was other times
other nights
     late
     in the late night
        like now

     when I was nobody
     thinking I was somebody
        living a fool's illusion

but life is a kiss
     kiss and tell

kiss and tell
and go to hell

drink
      drink yourself/myself into oblivion
it's the only safe/sacred ground

      the only pathway
      away from/to forget
         the chill

drink
         I have
         I will
         for nothing but
         absent reality
         will do

thirty-nine

and as every life
must come to an end
every dream
is bound by failure

you can buy a woman anything:
    clothing
    car(s)
    expensive watches

you can buy a woman everything
but her mother will still say
    this is nice
    but what about real life?

you can buy a woman all the things
for I have purchased most

you can give them all the possessions
but they will eventually become old

yes, you can
kill yourself
inside and out
buying objects
with money you do not have
buying them everything
but it is like giving them nothing
    who in the end
    is the fool

now, I have tried to buy the truth
paid too much for the lie(s)
      and the love(s)
and somehow these objects
have never been worth the price

      for something
      will forever
      equal nothing

money and love
they go hand-in-hand
they are forever intertwined

but lies lead to purchases
purchases hold the keys to the lies
and though I have tried
money has never bought me
my way out of any relationship

lost
it is such a poetic sounding word

alone
it reeks of freedom

lost and alone
hand-in-hand
     the road to misery

yes, I live in misery
returned to a city
     my city
chasing whatever illusion
there may be
     but I find none

late night
jetlag
feels like a bad hangover

     where am I to run
     who am I to love
     what is the medication for misery

another line of cocaine
another thought of nowhere left to run
but anywhere is better than here

lost
it is such a poetic sounding word

alone
it reeks of freedom

but they are words spoken
only to one's self

forty-two

I come home to no one
return from the great abyss
      asia
I come home to no one
I have come home
to this before

      deep lost
      months in china
      intertwined/interwoven
      women/love
      there I had it all
      here…
      I have nothing

I lay down the mirror
I sprinkle out the powder
      razor blade
      I finely chop it
      form it
      into a perfect line

      art
      chopping cocaine
         it is an art form

      the straw finds it way
      to my nose

I look down onto the mirror
that holds the magic
I see my reflection
I look up
into my large bathroom mirror
    the one above the bathroom sink
    I see my reflection again

    this is where I am working my magic
    inviting the magic
        yes, I pray to the devil
        the devil of the drink
        and of the line

    my bathroom
    where the magic
    is now being actualized
    when I think about it
    powdering my nose
    in my bathroom
    that is pretty strange

    but me
    I look up
    I look down
    again, I see my reflection
        double reflection

                    the mirror above
                    the mirror below

on a jetlag morning
with nothing left to loose
nowhere left to be
no one left to call
no one left to love
I embrace the touch of ecstasy
I let the powder caress my soul

the morning
screams at me
a morning
which I have never known
a morning
      the morning:
            a fool's passion
            a bohemian's sin

the morning comes on
leading from the night
      the night
      which is my friend
      the night
      which I know so well

      the night
      a bohemian's passionate daydream
      the mystic's elixir

jetlag
it still rages inside of me
like the nagging lingering
nondescript pain of a hangover
      alive
      but unfeeling
      touching
      but unknown

home
l.a.

me
I do not want to be home
      no longer does it hold
      its spell of illusion

s.e. asia
dirty
lust
modernized to a fault
      where the women's teeth are not clean
      the whites of their eyes
            slightly yellow
      slammed hard
            against the day
      slammed deep
            into the night

women…
with nothing left to loose
      like me/like her
like the whole situation

lost

I wait to leave home
to go home
to my new home
       it took me a long time
       a lot of journeys
       to realize it

       it took me a lot of years
       to know where I should be

here I sit
twenty-nine going on thirty

time to realize the realization
that l.a.
holds none of the haveable dreams
none of the promised illusions
none of the wanted reasons
why people like me
sneak out into the night

       go
       leave
       escape to the land of the lost
       the place
       where I long to return

cocaine
and jet lag

java
and awakening
      at the time
      I usually sleep

lust
confessed
poetry of a fool
where do I now go

      have I seen too much
      experienced too much
            to ever be normal again

      is there anyway
      left for me
            to go in
      is there anyway
      left for me
            to get out

me
tainted
beyond control

it is almost midnight
in bangkok
my two time zone
rolex tells me so

midnight
     the witching hour
midnight
     my time
midnight
     for all those with no reason
midnight
     the hour for those
          who have long ago
          left anything worth living behind

bangkok
what is it now
a week since I left her
bangkok
I wish I was back there again

bangkok
     where hell is evident
bangkok
     where hell is eminent
bangkok
     where hell is not hidden

l.a
I have returned to l.a.
    hidden
    hell
    is hidden
    here
        hidden
        but destructive
        hidden
        but stabbing like a knife
            in the heart
        hidden
        but too real
        to be unreal
        hidden
        but equipped with the insanity
        to destroy a mystic's soul

it is almost midnight
in bangkok
    if I had a dollar
    I would pack up
    and return to her today
        if I had a reason
        I would never leave her again
            if I had anything
            I would leave l.a. forever

time
time alone
killing time
     does it mean anything at all

stare into the t.v.
my eyes have a haze over them
     my mind dwells
     in the distance
        spaced distance
     space:
     it can be heave
     it can be hell
        point of view/state of mind

time
distance
life
     the time distance of life

lost
in a haveable world
lost
no where to go

distant
lost
time

and as the dream
calls out its wisdom
as the pressure
of the high
takes hold
as all of those
     ones like me
        who only say, *"yes."*
        never say, *"no."*
    those who know how to party
    party, past the point
the ones for whom
one is never enough
    come on
    come and walk with me

alone
with letters to write
babes on the telephone

alone
w/ women waiting all over the world
    but they just aren't full-on
    full-on like the fools
    full-on like me

full-on
the only truth

what am I thinking of
I am thinking of nothing
        ...drug induced nothing

where do I want to be
        no-where

what do I want to be
        no-one

drug induced nothing
        no-where
        no-one

freedom, is it?
        I don't know

what I do know is
        desire is hell
        life is a battle
        and a moment or three of nothing
                is always a welcomed relief

how are you felling?
about what
        I ask

can I come over tonight?

tonight
tonight
tonight
she has asked me that so many times
        some many time before

but don't you see
we live in different worlds
        I tell her

we live in different worlds...
that's because you never let me into your world

it's better that way, I think
...better that we keep it that way

            lost love
            and distant feelings
            lost all too long ago
            leave me to the lust
            it is where I seem to belong
            leave me to the alone

the alone
where I bath
in that tears
that so many have cried over me

lightening striking
in the distance
west
out over this ocean city

I sit still
awaiting…
a glass of vino in my hand

here it is clear
cloudy and clear
     there are stars
     over my head

me, I am lost
lost and asking for help
     help from the great beyond
but there is no help to be found

I wait
I watch
     one more for me
     one more chain lightening
        chain lightening strike
        it splits into two

I look to the north
I see an airplane taking off
    taking off to the west
    into the eye of the storm

    I long to move into its epicenter again

what did I do
    to earn this day
what did I do
    to achieve this moment of silence
what did I do
    to earn these lost/last words
        what did I do

as this moment ticks on
as the world ends its day
    as it comes down around me

    it comes down
        for all you who were once young
        and now are getting older
          like me

what have I done to achieve this

    as all those who claim to hold fast
    to their dream
        sell out
    as all those who claimed to be artist
        become waitresses/stewardesses
    me, I hold fast to the nothing

nothing
the perfect truth
nothing
the perfect reality

why have all the visions of others past
shattered in my face
gone
all those I believed
but they bought into the lie
instead of fighting for the truth

what did I do to deserve this day
what did I do to earn this day

have you seen the wind wander
have you felt the tears of the sky
have you known a feeling
      any feeling at all

if you have
then you know
it changes you
      forever
      and ever

have you ever seen the dreamers fail
      where they ever dreamers at all
have you ever cried
alone in the night
      for what you have
      for what you don't have

      what you thought you knew
      and never knew

      it passes on:
          life
          death
          words
          and wisdom
      for a second it is here
      and then it is gone

has the night ever kissed you
     for if it has
     then you will never be the same

has the dream ever alluded you
     if it has
     then you know the source of:
          anguish
          frustration
          pain

so dance your dance
as so few ever know how to dream
dream your dream
as even fewer cast their dreams to reality

god, I'm fucked up
fucked up
and fucked over
my brain feels like scrambled eggs

    should I do some more coke
        to pick me up
    or some valiums
        to take me down

out my door
over my patio
the world spins on the beach
    people play
    people laugh
    people darken their skin
    but that is just not me

me, I like it at thirty-nine thousand feet
    first-class
        drink, ice coffee

me, I like s.e. asia
where life is just so haveable
    and the heat
    it has no reason

yes, it is hot today
even here at the beach
summer is in full bloom
        I am out of my element
I guess that has always been the case

        lust
        where do I go
        lust
        what do I do

drugs:
god, I'm fucked up
fucked up
and fucked over
my brain feels like scrambled eggs

        should I do some more coke
                to pick me up
        or some valiums
                to take me down

fifty-four

I embarked on a journey
    screaming for the dream

I returned home
    older
    wiser
    and still screaming

I look across my living room
      drafting table up against the wall
        I paint
        I write there

    letters of love
    love letters
    letters of lies
        past and present
        memories
    women who I loved
    women who loved me
        there they are
        written words of promises
        written words of wonderment

            more letters
            from more places
            than I have ever received

in any other
given period of time

and I realize
the journey/that journey is not over
it continues
and I still scream for the dream

the sun is setting
on this california seascape
I sit on my patio
     on *the strand*
from a nearby
     within earshot
home
     plays loud music
     by a lousy rock band

     I wish they would stop
     their entertainment
     is not desired

I would prefer to only hear
the ever-caressing sound of the ocean
but her magic is interrupted
by annoying, loud, and bad musicians

I never understood
why people have to bring
artificial stimuli
into the realms of the natural
     the mystical

fifty-six

I took a late night drive to long beach
      top down
      radio on

I listened to some heavy metal station
from san diego

then I stopped at a supermarket
on my way home

and now I prepare what I purchased
      hot chocolate

so I am going to dowse down that
have it with tons of whip crème
and then I'm going to go to bed
and try to pretend that I don't hurt so much inside
and that it doesn't matter
that I haven't written all the books
that I have inside of me

fifty-seven

I wake up
lay in bed for an hour or two
no place to be
nothing to do

      lost and all alone

finally
I pull myself out
take a shower
catch a shave
promise to work on the many books
      I have in progress
promise to eat
      breakfast, lunch, dinner
         and push some accomplishment

well maybe…

maybe I should just get into these slow mornings
      maybe dream
      and go passively insane
      maybe do nothing

for all the pressure I give myself
maybe my life will add up to nothing at all

maybe it/my life
will all just pass

this life will be gone
      in the blink of an eye
and nothing will equal anything

maybe
I don't know

three cups of java down
    one
    two
    never do anything for me

    decaffeinated
    why bother

give me the rush
give me the feeling
give me anything
but nothing

    my computer
    it is turned on
    ready to word process away

me, I sit out here on my patio
staring at the waves
staring at the people
and watching the world go by

I should go and type
    type
    my never-ending autobiography
    of love, lust, desire, spirituality
    and the lot

but my mind
drifts to distant silence
and it all seems
just so much easier
to sit here and stare

so damn me
        if I am wrong
I'd be dammed
        even if I am right

and people
they tell me
        I should be careful
                careful to not drift too far away
                not to step too far beyond the realms
                of the normal/the accepted

but careful
        is for the old
careful
        is for the children

the old and the children
they each have something to loose
        not me

careful in not in my vocabulary

      accomplishment
          what does it mean
    in a world where dreams
        are lived in and out
            dreams reign supreme

in this world/in my world
the dreams are dreamed

the pain of fear
stabs my life
I have nowhere to run
and no one to turn to

I could go out
go out for a drive
        in a topless jeep
or I could stay home
        drink some more wine
        cry some more tears
        and wish
        my life
        had turned out
        another way

I am scared
I am lost
and worst of all
I am alone

sixty

I hear the people
they are partying outside
me,
       I am home alone
           again

I promised myself
I wouldn't be here
      on this birthday
          the 4th of july
birthday
u.s. style

      but money…
      the lack of

      but life…
      and adverse destiny
          they hold me
          in this country

free?
independence?
me?
      times they do change

so I sit here
    alone
    wishing
    again

this is not the way I would have created it
    life
    noise
    the people outside
        it is too deafening

I resort again
to the tempering of the wine

the world makes noise around me
I couldn't sleep
even if I wanted to
so I sit down
at the typing keys
produce words
to be read by the masses

> the masses…
> who would/will never read a word
> no, not a word I write
>
> they never read
> > …not a word
> > written by one of us
>
> us…
> who scream so politically incorrectly
> in the night
>
> the masses…
> those…
> them…
> > who earn an honorable living
>
> the masses...
> those…
> them…
> > who never step outside

never step outside
and see the light

the masses...
those…
them…
          who choose to only make noise
          when it is acceptable/palatable

the masses...
those…
them…
          who make the noise in my life
                    now

this/them
that cause me
to sit down
in my semi drunken state
and type at the typing keys
for a people
who would/could never possess the vision
to read the words I write

and the daybreak breaks dreams
and all I can do is think of you

yeah, ten thousand miles away
you
you and I
lifetimes apart

    dream
as the sun rises
    dream
in the sunset
    dream
as I fly away
       fly away to a never know land
       a land
       that you will never know

dreams
and distance
as the morning
kisses my eyes
just as you used to kiss my lips
in the morning
     mornings
    a lifetime ago
and the daybreak breaks dreams
and all I can do is think of you

sixty-three

I lay down on my couch
I want to shut the world out
I want to turn off the tears
        that ring in my ears
cried by my not to distant babe
over the telephone lines

        she thinks I am something
        something that I am
        she thinks I have something to offer her
        I wish I did
        but I don't

I lay down on my couch
the voices of those on summer break at the ocean
        whisper outside
                they haunt my ears

I want to run away
but where is there no place left to go

I am so sorry that she cries
I am so sorry that she blames me
        for something
                that is not my fault
I am so sorry for my dysfunctional inadequacies
        as an individual
        as a human being

I am so sorry for all the things that I am not

I want to sleep
lay down on my couch
and run deeply away
      someplace where it doesn't hurt
      someplace where the poetry I have to write
          is written
      someplace where the art is live
        and the music is played
      someplace where I have the chance
            the chance
            that has never been given

      somewhere/anywhere

and yes, I love you
my sweet little west hollywood
glam slam girl
yes, I love you
      when this is not that
        only this

      I love you
      when we are alone
      holding each other
      in the pure magic
      of the no outside

but you cry because you want things
things which I can not give
things that I do not have
            money
            support
            a house
            a home
            all of your bills paid
the list you make is long

but what does a dream do
what can it be but a dream
how can I be anything
other than what I am
            an illusion

and you make me feel like so much less
by loving you

            life spins
            wheels turn
            dreams dissipate
            and happiness slips away

I lay down on my couch
I want to shut the world out

in too deep
in too deep again
     same woman
     different time
     same magic
     different lies

and if I were more
I would not have let myself
fall back into her arms

and if I was not so alone
I would not have let myself
fall back under her love's control

     I love her
     but it hurts to love her

     it is magic
     but the price is so high

       in too deep
           again

sixty-five

I didn't like today
I didn't like it since 12:00 PM
    too much anger
    too much jealousy
    too much unhappiness
    too much of nothing
I did not like today

now you left me to pick up the pieces again
      she says to me on the telephone line

she
my main
west hollywood
glam slam
taiwan princess
      who I thought
      I would never see again

but me…
my life is strange...
unexpected/unplanned
we turned and walked
      face-to-face
right into each other
in a mass of people
in a massive city
in a massive world
      and she would not let me walk away

so a moment turns into a day
a day turns into a night
      and in the night
      we do make love
         that girl could fuck
but then a night turns into another day

another day into another week
and another week into oblivion
 going nowhere
 nowhere to nowhere

and I give
she takes

again, I exit, stage left

so you gave me an empty promise again
 so she cries on the telephone line

what are empty promises to a liar
 I hang up

now
the beach is empty
I look out
and the laughing crowds have gone
    they are gone
    gone
    gone to the palaces of wonder
    their realms of safety
        places where the timeless
        realms of mysticism
        do not dwell
it has become quiet now
my mind is empty
I look out onto placid pacific freedom

    gone
        the woman who
        haunts my life
        loves my life
        taunts my life
    gone
        to where the passion
        it is not so strong
        to where the essence
        is not so fierce

           and life
           is so much easier lived

About the Author

Scott Shaw is a prolific author, actor, filmmaker, photographer, and composer. Shaw's poetry and literary fiction were first published by literary journals in the late 1970s. He continued forward to have several works of poetry and literary fiction published, in book form, during the 1980s. By the mid 1980s, after having spent years traveling extensively throughout Asia, documenting obscure aspects of Asian culture in words and on film, his writings on social science began to be published, as well. As the 1990s dawned, Shaw writings, based upon a lifelong involvement with the martial arts and eastern mysticism, began to be embraced. From this, he has authored hundreds of articles and numerous books on meditation, the martial arts, yoga, and Zen Buddhism; published by large publishing houses.

Books by Scott Shaw include:

About Peace: A 108 Ways to Be At Peace When Things Are Out of Control
Advanced Taekwondo
Bangkok and the Nights of Drunken Stupor
Cambodian Refugees in Long Beach, California: The Definitive Study
Chi Kung For Beginners
China Deep
Essence: The Zen of Everything
Hapkido: Articles on Self-Defense
Hapkido: Essays on Self-Defense
Hapkido: The Korean Art of Self-Defense
Independent Filmmaking: Secrets of the Craft
Junk: The Backstreets of Bangkok
Last Will and Testament According to the Divine Rite of the Drug Cocaine
L.A.: Tales from the Suburban Side of Hell
Marguerite Duras and Charles Bukowski: The Yin and Yang of Modern Erotic Literature
Mastering Health: The A to Z of Chi Kung
Nirvana in a Nutshell
On the Hard Edge of Hollywood
Sake' in a Glass, Sushi with Your Fingers: Fifteen Minutes in Tokyo
Samurai Zen
Shanghai Whispers Shanghai Screams
Shattered Thoughts
Suicide Slowly
Taekwondo Basics
The Ki Process: Korean Secrets for Cultivating Dynamic Energy
The Little Book of Yoga Breathing
The Little Book of Zen Mediation

The Most Beautiful Woman in Shanghai
The Passionate Kiss of Illusion
The Screenplays
The Tao of Chi
The Tao of Self Defense
The Warrior is Silent:
The Zen of Modern Life and the Reality of Reality
Martial Arts and the Spiritual Path
TKO: A Lost Night in Tokyo
Yoga: The Spiritual Aspects
Zen Buddhism: The Pathway to Nirvana
Zen Filmmaking
Zen in the Blink of an Eye
Zen O'clock: Time to Be
Zen: Tales from the Journey

www.ingramcontent.com/pod-product-compliance
Lightning Source LLC
Chambersburg PA
CBHW052107090426
42741CB00009B/1715